HEADSTART HISTORY PAPERS

Thomas Cromwell

by

Geoffrey Elton

HEADSTART HISTORY

Published by	HEADSTART HISTORY PO Box 41, Bangor, Gwynedd, LL57 1SB
Set by	THE WORDSMITH GROUP The Manor House, Tarvin, Chester
Printed by	THE IPSWICH BOOK COMPANY LTD The Drift, Nacton Road, Ipswich, Suffolk IP3 3QR

ISBN   1 873041 15 2

A CIP catalogue record for this book is available from the British Library

CONTENTS

Introduction

Further reading

Bibliography of Geoffrey Elton

Frontispiece: Thomas Cromwell
                  by Holbein
                  Copyright The Frick Collection,
                       New York

CONTENTS

INTRODUCTION

The HEADSTART HISTORY PAPERS aim to identify important themes and topics the signifigance of which extends beyond the studies of professional historians. The PAPERS are distillations of the research of distinguished scholars in a form appropriate to sixth formers, undergraduates and the general reader.

Geoffrey Elton began his work on Thomas Cromwell in 1946. His thesis was submitted in 1948 and five years later he published THE TUDOR REVOLUTION IN GOVERNMENT, a book which became a landmark to scholars of Tudor history and gave rise to vigorous debate.

The issues which Geoffrey Elton raised in that book were developed in a series of learned articles, in the Ford Lectures given at Oxford in 1971 and in the Wiles Lectures given in Belfast in 1972. The former were published in POLICY AND POLICE and the latter in REFORM AND RENEWAL. In Belfast the lectures presented Cromwell not just as a legislator but as a social reformer, an intellectual and an idealist. This controversial view suggesting a politician of conscience and vision aroused further debate on the nature of the English Reformation and that in turn produced a revived interest in the Pilgrimage of Grace and the reasons for Thomas Cromwell's fall from power.

Fruitful discussion over the years led Geoffrey Elton to modify his interpretation of events and those views were presented in REFORM AND REFORMATION in 1977. Thereafter his interests shifted to constitutional issues of the later period and that work was published in THE PARLIAMENT OF ENGLAND, 1559-1581.

ENGLAND UNDER THE TUDORS and THE TUDOR CONSTITUTION are established textbooks which have been used by successive generations of sixth formers and undergraduates. In this PAPER Geoffrey Elton sets out the essence of his thoughts on Thomas Cromwell and the challenge to which those thoughts have been subject.

Geoffrey Elton retired from the Regius Chair of Modern History at Cambridge in 1988 but he has certainly not retired from historical scholarship. As Editor of the HEADSTART HISTORY PAPERS I would like to record my personal gratitude to Sir Geoffrey for agreeing to present the first PAPER in the series.

JUDITH LOADES,
Bangor, 1990.

THOMAS CROMWELL

I

Thomas Cromwell was born round about the year 1485, at Putney or Wimbledon in the county of Surrey where his father Walter worked as a shearman and alehouse-keeper. His lifespan thus began in step with the arrival of the Tudors on the throne. He seems to have been the youngest of his parent's children and the least obedient as well; as he was later to tell Cranmer, in his young days he had been a bit of a ruffian. The connection with the noble family of Cromwell of Tattershall, which has sometimes been suspected, would seem to be entirely imaginary. Walter Cromwell was a man with whom it proved difficult to live in peace, and in his late teens Thomas took off for the continent. He crossed to the Netherlands and from there wandered through France into Italy, allegedly - and the story is by no means beyond the bounds of possibility - serving as a soldier in the wars there; he is said to have fought in the French army in the battle of the Garigliano (December 1503). Certainly he later showed some direct and fairly unusual understanding of the French military strength and system. However, he got out of the wars as quickly as possible and turned to trade. He took service with a Venetian servant; in 1513 he stayed briefly at the English Hospice in Rome; then he made his way north again. In 1514 he is found dealing on his own behalf in the northern mercantile capital of Antwerp. Thereafter he returned to his native country, having acquired not only very varied experiences but also several languages. Back home, he married Elizabeth Wykys, daughter of another shearman but from a family which had connections with the court of Henry VII; of the children of the marriage only a boy, Gregory, lived beyond childhood. His travelling days, however, were not entirely over: in 1517 and 1518, he twice led an embassy to Rome, organised by the town of Boston (Lincs.) for the purpose of obtaining a bull of indulgence from Pope Leo X. Apart from the fact that he used the journey to learn the New Testament by heart (or so John Foxe tells us), this trip to Rome must have been something of a holiday for one who had been in service with Cardinal Wolsey since 1516.[1]

Actually, Cromwell's connection with Boston seems to have arisen out of his private activities in trade and the law; he knew a leading man of those parts, John Robinson, well and corresponded with him quite regularly.[2] And it was Robinson, alderman of Boston, who had been instrumental in founding the guild for whose necessary documents Cromwell went to Rome, but Boston was more remote from his normal centre of action than his usual contacts, most of them in London. Once Cromwell had returned from the continent he settled down to a career of private enterprise and built up a flourishing practice especially in the law from his residence in Fenchurch Street (later he moved to a house in Stepney). By the early 1520s he was very active indeed in quite a range of courts. Thus, in October 1520 he acted in an appeal from the prerogative court of Canterbury to the Roman Curia, and early in 1522

---

1 Cf. R. B. Merriman, *Life and Letters of Thomas Cromwell* (Oxford, 1902), i, 5ff., and G. R. Elton, *Studies in Tudor and Stuart Politics and Government* (3 vols., Cambridge, 1974, 1983), iii, 373-5.

2 *Letters and Papers ... of the Reign of Henry VIII* (hereafter *LP*), iii, 3015. Robinson sat regularly on local commissions of gaol delivery, of the peace, of sewers and for the subsidy (ibid. 1081[26], 278[18] and 2587[22], 1379[16], and p. 1457).

he served as attorney for a litigant from Bristol in a case before the Council in Star Chamber.[3] But the bulk of his business, then and later, lay in the common law.[4] By the middle of 1522, the shearman's son had risen in wealth and standing sufficiently to merit description as gentleman in a power of attorney granted by a merchant of the German Hanse,[5] and in 1524 he became a member of Gray's Inn, thus testifying to his standing in the English legal profession.

These private enterprises went on until the early 1530s, but long before that date Cromwell had entered upon what was to be his real career. As has been said, by 1516 he had joined the household of Thomas Wolsey, cardinal and lord chancellor, and ruler of England under Henry VIII; by 1519 at the latest he had become a member of the cardinal's council.[6] How Wolsey got to hear of him, or how Cromwell attracted the cardinal's attention, remains uncertain; the notion that as late as 1522 he was in the service of Henry Grey, marquess of Dorset, rests upon two undatable letters which in fact indicate no more than that the Grey family may have been among his business clients. Now that we can place him in Wolsey's service within two years of his return and his marriage we know at least that for some fifteen years, by the side of his private practice, he served the cardinal as a councillor and counsellor. By

---

3 Ibid. iii, 1026, 1963.

4 E.g. ibid. 2441, 2445, 2557, 3081, etc.

5 Ibid. 447.

6 Elton, *Studies*, iii, 374 n.6.

the end of the decade he was clearly the chancellor's chief lay assistant; more particularly he had acquired experience which later proved useful when he superintended the dissolution of several small religious houses whose endowment Wolsey diverted to the foundation of his school at Ipswich and his college at Oxford (later refounded by Henry VIII as Christ Church). Wolsey's entourage bred up numbers of able administrators, many of them transferred in due course to the king's service while others joined Cromwell's private office after Wolsey's fall. It was the most promising and satisfactory training ground for men of ambition.

In 1523, Cromwell took yet another step into the public life of the realm: he became a member of the Commons in the Parliament called in that year, mainly to supply the money needed for Wolsey's aggressive foreign policy. We do not know which seat he sat for, but we do have a piece of evidence somewhat exceptional for that age - the draft of a speech which he probably delivered in the obviously acrimonious debates around the crown's financial demands.[7] In a delicate mixture of firm loyalty and serious criticism, Cromwell ventured to cast grave doubt on Henry VIII's favourite pose as an heir to the martial greatness of England's medieval kings. He explained that the country could not afford the expenditure which pretensions to the crown of France involved and strikingly demonstrated his personal understanding of conditions in that country when he met the regularly implied memories of Crécy and Agincourt with up-to-date information on the military strength of France. He also suggested that

---

7 Merriman, i, 30-44. There is little reason to doubt that the speech, written out in the hand of one of Cromwell's clerks, was delivered.

England had better concentrate on the threat posed by Scottish hostility on her northern border: before immersing herself in continental adventure she would do well to complete her security in the island. It is possible that Cromwell was put up by Wolsey to prepare the ground for change in policy,[8] but rather more likely that he was trying to arrest a mistaken policy in mid-flight: the tone of the speech supports the second interpretation rather than the first.

What really comes across in the speech is a penetrating view of reality put forth with exceptional powers of oratory. Even if we did not know of Cromwell's later career, we should here recognize a man of special competence, a statesman not so much in the making as already made. Nor is it altogether meaningless that those qualities should have first appeared on the stage of the House of Commons. After the Parliament of 1523 had gone home, Cromwell wrote a letter to a close friend then abroad, actually the first of his letters to survive.[9] He knew that his correspondent, John Croke, would wish to hear the latest news from home. 'for it is said that news refreshes the spirit of life'.

> Wherefore ye shall understand that by long time I amongst other have endured a Parliament which continued by the space of sixteen whole weeks, where we communed of war, peace, strife, contention, debate, murmur, grudge, riches, poverty, truth, falsehood, justice, equity, deceit,

---

8 John Guy in *Law and Government under the Tudors*, ed. C. Cross, D. Loades, J. J. Scarisbrick (Cambridge, 1988), 15-16.

9 Merriman, i, 313-14.

> oppression, magnanimity, activity, force, attemperance, treason, murder, felony, conciliation, and also how a commonwealth might be edified and also continued within our realm. Howbeit, in conclusion we have done as our predecessors have been wont to do, that is to say, as well as we might and left as we began.

This splendidly amused and amusing review of the buzzing futility of much public life has often been read, by owlish historians anxious to trounce the clear-headed realist with the baubles of liberal earnestness, as contempt for all Parliaments. On the contrary, it shows that Cromwell fully understood how such assemblies operate, and it forecasts the efficient manager who a decade later was to manoeuvre Parliament into doing something about many of the issues here touched upon.

The recipient of this letter, then resident at Bilbao, has left us evidence of one aspect of our man which has been habitually overlooked. In July of the previous year (1522), Croke had sent a letter full of truly passionate devotion to Thomas Cromwell - the letter of a deeply attached friend.[10] Cromwell, in fact, had a genius for friendship - and I do mean friendship, not mere acquaintance. During those last years of domestic peace he lived in a London community of closeknit and frequent intercourse, and his circle of relations included not only his and his wife's families[11] but also the leading merchants of the City, the

---

10 *LP* iii, 2394.

11 He gave a roof over her head to his mother-in-law after his wife died in 1527.

circle of Sir Thomas More and John Rastell (where, it would seem, he on occasion played bowls), and especially the Genoese merchant Antonio Bonvisi, close friend to both More and Cromwell. Cromwell's gift for friendship rested upon a strikingly consistent loyalty to such ties once they had been formed; in later life, when he had become the man in and of power, he remained notorious for never forgetting old friends or rejecting people who in their day had done him a kindness, no matter how lowly or uninfluential they might be. Above all, that quality of loyalty was called forth by the disaster that now befell the man to whose fortune he had tied his own. In October 1529 Wolsey suddenly fell from power, and for a time it looked as though Cromwell might lose all he had built up.

II

Cromwell's first reaction to Wolsey's fall was a mixture of stunned disbelief and near despair. George Cavendish, Wolsey's gentleman-usher and biographer, found the cardinal's solicitor in a window embrasure in Wolsey's place at Esher, reading 'our Lady's matins - which had been a strange sight in him afore', with the tears rolling down his cheeks. He was confronting the collapse of all he had worked for in making a success of a life that had started so unpromisingly, and he had good reason to fear that he might be used as Wolsey's scapegoat. However, that uncharacteristic black mood did not last long. After advising Wolsey on the winding up of his excessive establishment, he went off to London, with his master's permission, to, as he put it, 'make or mar'. The Parliament which Henry had summoned to cope with the collapse of Wolsey's policy and his own intended divorce from Catherine of Aragon, opened on 3 November 1529, and the day before Cromwell had put out various feelers to establish contacts in promising quarters. In the end he was belatedly returned as one of the members of Taunton (a seat in the gift of the bishop of Winchester, still one of Wolsey's sees), and his real public career had begun. He had first made sure that Henry would approve of his entering the Parliament, in expectation of his services there. This choice of Parliament as the stage from which to secure immunity against hostile attacks and launch political action was highly innovatory: Cromwell turned out to be the first statesman in English history who built his rise to power on membership of the House of Commons.

Not that such membership could by itself lead to power; Cromwell needed to gain the attention of the king and indeed needed formally to enter the royal service. The really impressive thing about his switch from Wolsey to Henry, however, lies in the delay that supervened. Shoals of Wolsey's servants immediately washed their hands of their old master and rushed to join the service of the crown, none more eagerly than Stephen Gardiner (Cromwell's junior by a dozen years) who almost immediately changed from being Wolsey's secretary to becoming Henry's and as soon as Wolsey was gone acquired the see of Winchester, the wealthiest in England. Cromwell, on the other hand, followed his entrenched instinct of loyalty and continued to look after Wolsey and his affairs until the cardinal died. Those affairs - more particularly the disposal of the lands confiscated for the now abolished school at Ipswich and the preservation of the Oxford college - certainly gave him a chance to establish contact with court and courtiers; he also demonstrated his general managerial abilities in quarters where their recognition would prove useful. But his service remained attached to Wolsey, continuing the ties of some fifteen years. He used his seat in the Commons to talk out an attempt to pass a bill of attainder against the fallen minister, and he kept a careful eye on feelings at court about a man who, though no longer in power, seemed very unwilling to accept that his days of glory had gone. Cromwell's letters grew ever more urgent, even desperate, in his efforts to make Wolsey recognise reality. Just when he became the king's servant is not quite clear, but there is no good evidence of this transfer till just after Wolsey's death in November 1530. Cromwell did not desert his old master in his days of dire trouble, even though continuing to serve Wolsey could be an exasperating experience and involved risks for his own future.

Once Wolsey was gone, Cromwell was able to give his time to the construction of his new career. Not his whole time: his private legal practice continued spasmodically for some years, and even when affairs of state crowded his agenda old friendships and obligations incurred were nor forgotten. But from early in 1531 he showed himself active in the service of Henry VIII and was soon addressed as a member of the royal Council. To all appearance, he remained for a time very much a lesser member of that body and was mainly employed in legal business, until by the end of the year he emerged as one of the king's leading councillors, especially responsible for conducting the king's business in Parliament. Henry, generally a good judge of men though less of women, had taken the measure of his new recruit, and for the next eight years Cromwell commanded ever more authority in the governing and refashioning of the realm.

The man who had arrived at this leading role in the history of England was about forty-five years old - well into middle age by the standards of the time and making a rather late start in public life. We have only one decent portrait of him - or rather, the only decent portrait is a contemporary copy of a painting by Hans Holbein, made about 1532. It shows a man of middling height and solid body, with a large face, small prying eyes, and a general air of reserve. What it does not show is the brilliant conversationalist and intellectually exciting operator that much comment shows him to have been. Determined, long-sighted, potentially relentless, but also of ready wit, accommodating in social intercourse, and profoundly interested in matters of first principle, he proved himself an agile performer but always in the service of major causes. He brought to the royal service and the governance of England an experience that was really unique. None of Henry's other ministers or agents had lived so long at the bottom of the social pyramid, had made his way so exclusively by his own abilities without the frequent benefits of family or patronage, or had survived the collapse of his only patron so very much by his own efforts and without betraying the trust reposed in him. He knew Italy, France and the Netherlands at first hand, and though how he acquired all his languages must remain mysterious he proved fluent enough in French, Italian and Latin. He knew much law and all about England's foreign trade, and service under Wolsey had taught him much about the management of landed estates; he had acquired a considerable understanding of the state of the Church and the monasteries; and within a short time he acquired a reasonable mastery of the factions of Council and Court. Yet he still lacked the close contacts with what are usually regarded as the true centres of power, that is the inner reaches of that Court; more especially he had not yet formed any alliance with the up-and-coming interest, with Anne Boleyn and her family. He had had no formal education, not even in the law; to a most unusual degree he had fashioned his own mind and career, and to a degree he continued to depend on himself. And on his king, of course: a fair start but also one full of risk and future uncertainty. So long as Henry backed him he was virtually irresistible - while Henry backed him.

III

The battle for ascendancy in the king's Council, which began with the fall of Wolsey, ended in May 1532 with, in effect, a victory for Cromwell. That victory was announced in the acceptance by the Convocation of the Clergy of the principle that the law of the Church would in future depend on the consent of the king, in the same way as secular laws required his assent in Parliament, and the decisive moment came when this event secured the resignation of Sir Thomas More, Wolsey's successor as chancellor and the determined champion of the Universal Church of Rome. The place of this last defender of the Church's independence was taken by Thomas Audley, lately speaker of the House of Commons and thereafter Cromwell's chief assistant in the management of Parliament and the preparation of new legislation. For the next eight years Cromwell dominated the government of the realm, though he never lacked rivals and enemies; while he could never afford to copy the autocratic habits of his late master, he was in any case constitutionally inclined to work by persuasion, cooperation and flexibility. Above all, as he knew well, he could never take Henry's support for granted, even though urgency of business often compelled him to act in anticipation of it; by this time no one in public affairs any longer doubted the king's dangerous readiness to resolve any difficulty by finding a scapegoat. However, immediately Cromwell commanded Henry's favour and trust, as the offices testified that he rapidly gathered in. Some provided influence on lesser aspects of the administration and only modest rewards, but several gave him very wide powers. Though it was only in April 1534 that he formally replaced Stephen Gardiner as principal secretary he effectively carried out the functions of that office from the spring of 1532 onwards as Gardiner lost favour over the Submission of the Clergy and was shunted into embassies abroad. Though Cromwell ruled everything as Master Secretary, the inevitable elevation to the peerage in June 1536 as Lord Cromwell of Wimbledon also called for a more eminent office and was combined with his appointment as lord privy seal in succession to the earl of Wiltshire, the loser in the faction fight which cost the life of his daughter, Queen Anne Boleyn. Along the way Cromwell had also picked up the mastership of the rolls (which extended his influence over the great seal and the court of Chancery), and in January 1535 he became vicar-general and vicegerent in spirituals, that is to say, the king's deputy as ruler of the spiritualty. The earldom of Essex and the great chamberlaincy of the Household which came his way on the eve of his fall signified something in the political struggles of his last few months but did not in any way increase his standing and powers. Cromwell, pluralist in office-holding, treated none of his appointments, major or minor, as sinecures; on the occasions that he wished to free himself from the work involved he passed on office and fees to someone else. Above everything else, he was a worker, indefatigably so.[12]

---

12 For Cromwell's offices and his use of them, cf. G. R. Elton, *The Tudor Revolution in Government* (Cambridge, 1953), 98-159. The vicegerency took longer to become a complete delegation of the royal supremacy than used to be thought; originally confined to the running of a total visitation of the Church it was fully expanded in July 1536: F. D. Logan, 'Thomas Cromwell and the Vicegerency in Spirituals: a

The 1530s turned out to be a period of much change and almost feverish activity; it is not too much to say that most aspects of life in England and her dependencies underwent major alteration in this decade, often behind a pretence of continuity. The scene was set by Henry VIII's first divorce - by his desire to jettison his first wife, Catherine of Aragon, and marry Anne Boleyn. Wolsey fell because he could not secure a lawful ending to the first marriage, and he could not do so because he remained committed to the rule of the papacy over the Church. Henry's problems were solved when earlier assertions that such matters should properly be dealt with locally, in whatever sector of the Church was in question, and without interference from Rome, became reality in the hands of a government which took the English Church right out of the papal allegiance. The instrument employed in turning claims into fact was the Parliament - the king-in-Parliament - treated as the sovereign maker of law for all concerns of the realm of England including the affairs of the Church; the legislation of the Reformation Parliament (1529-1536) progressed from the anticlerical threats of 1529 through the banning of appeals to courts outside the realm (1533) to the codification of the Royal Supremacy over the Church and the definition of its legal and administrative powers. Most of these acts were drafted by Cromwell and all passed the Commons under his management, while his ally Thomas Audley presided over the Lords.

The years of Cromwell's activity witnessed thereafter a great number of changes, all of them highly significant in their implications even if not all of them were brought to

---

revisitation,' *Eng. Hist. Rev.* 103 (1988), 658-67.

a conclusion. The demand for the divorce produced the assertion that England was an empire, a united and unitary realm free from all foreign control and organised as both state and Church under one person, both king and supreme head. This 'break with Rome' needed to be widely publicised and enforced against possible and actual opposition, work which required a ceaseless output of information and propaganda backed up by the maintenance of an enforcement network constructed from the traditional relationships between the rulers of the shires and their people on the one hand, and the king's officers on the other.[13] Furthermore, the constitutional revolution in the Church let loose an increasing desire for a reform in religion, a desire which drew strength both from indigenous discontent with the spiritual state of the Church and from the mounting influence of the continental Reformation, both Lutheran and Swiss. The resignation of Thomas More for a time terminated anything like a consistent policy of persecution aimed against the innovators, and with the appointment of Thomas Cranmer as archbishop of Canterbury in January 1533 - a choice determined by the desire to find a Church leader willing to organise the divorce - the Reformation in religion by stages took charge of the ecclesiastical leadership. The attack on Church and priesthood found additional ammunition in the age-old desire on the part of king and landowners for some at least of the vast properties of the Church, and in 1535-1539 Cromwell superintended the dissolution of the monasteries and the transfer of their possessions to the crown. Further inroads on ecclesiastical lands were contemplated but not at this time carried out.

---

13 See G. R. Elton, *Policy and Police* (Cambridge, 1972).

The subjugation of the Church was by no means the only aspect of the unitary realm towards which this generation laboured. Traditional and well established rights vested in franchises were effectively legislated out of existence. Wales was brought within the normal shire system of the realm; Wales and Calais were given representation in Parliament to signify effective incorporation; and a very serious attempt to extend these principles also to Ireland failed only because it proved to be beyond the physical powers of the monarchy.[14] Within England, the government of the regions distant from London came to be more tightly organised under the ultimate supervision of the central Council and the principal secretary, nor should the fact that by no means all these efforts bore immediate fruit allow one to underestimate the efforts made.

These upheavals made the 1530s a very unpeaceful decade, a characteristic further strengthened by Henry's continued search for a contented marriage which added to the disturbing effects of political faction struggles at court. The glory of Anne Boleyn did not long survive her crowning, and when she failed to produce the male heir for whose sake Henry had started the whole business she, and with her a large court faction, was doomed (January-May 1536). Cromwell managed to survive this further disaster among his allies and even used it to shunt the conservative factions into the sidelines, but their rage led them to organise the disaffection current in the north of the country into a major rebellion, the Pilgrimage of Grace, which towards the end of 1536 threatened not only Cromwell's

---

14 Cf. Brendan Bradshaw, *The Irish Constitutional Revolution of the Sixteenth Century* (Cambridge, 1979), and S. G. Ellis, 'Thomas Cromwell and Ireland, 1532-1540,' *Hist. Journal* 23 (1980), 497-519.

position but Henry's very rule. The threat was beaten off and the decade rolled on, with further rumbling of revolt running alongside the manifest (though patchy) progress of the new religion encouraged from above, until the court battles culminated in the fall of Cromwell, about which more in a moment.

Two less political developments accompanied all this uproar. In the first place, both circumstances and policy promoted widespread administrative reform designed to improve control over public finance, strengthen the centralisation of government (the emergence of the secretary of state as the chief executive of the realm), and reconstruct the king's Council into a more efficient instrument of rule.[15] Secondly, the air resounded with demands for social and economic improvement: plans for reform of the law, of the rights and practices of landowners, concerning manufacture and trade, and for improving the lot of the poor piled up in the principal secretary's office; some at least got as far as bills and even acts in Parliament.[16] For one of the most striking facts about this decade was the renovation, as it were, of the sovereign law-making institution. The break with Rome had demonstrated that the unitary state acknowledged not only a single royal ruler, imperial in his crown, but also a single legislative sovereign who was the king linked with the Lords and the Commons in the Parliament. Even though by that time this institution already had some 250 years of life behind it, it changed both character and role

15 For the details see my *Tudor Revolution in Government*.

16 For details see G. R. Elton, *Reform and renewal: Thomas Cromwell and the Common Weal* (Cambridge, 1973), esp. chs. 5 and 6.

in this decade, a decade which witnessed its entry upon its post-medieval career. A rival institution, the more or less representative Great Council still summoned for political debate several times in the reign of Henry VII, vanished in the 1530s.[17] Frequency of meetings, massive production of enactments, regular managerial attention to its doings, all testified to its incorporation in the government of the realm from which it never again retreated into the somewhat ineffectual displays of bad temper which had become its chief characteristic since about 1370. And although it was not primarily an arena for political debate (as the medieval Parliament had often been), a more purposeful form of this function, contributing to government policy, can also be discerned in the 1530s - for the first time on points of principle unaffected by the interests of a dominant and narrow-minded aristocracy. Along with the promotion of parliamentary activity marched a determined modernisation of the common law of England, designed both too offer answers to current problems and to equip it for a sole rule in the realm at the expense of other rival laws.[18] The 1530s belonged to that category of ages - perhaps fortunately not all that common - when all sorts of well established rights, claims and convictions find themselves challenged on fundamental grounds. It was an age of reform, in intent, in action, and also (as usual) in suffering.

---

17 Cf. P. J. Holmes, 'The Great Council in the Reign of Henry VII,' *Eng. Hist. Rev.* 101 (1986), 30-52, and 'The Last Tudor Great Councils,' *Hist Journal*, 33 (1990), 1-22.

18 J. H. Baker, *The Reports of Sir John Spelman*, vol. 2 (Selden Society, 1978), pp. *23-346*.

IV

Opinions may differ about the size of the cataclysm that shook England in that decade and re-echoed thereafter for at least another generation, but that something pretty drastic and dramatic was going on is denied by hardly anyone. After all, the point was determinedly made by that hero of conservative reaction, Thomas More. What remains in dispute are, up to a point, the suddenness and precise effects of the change, as well as very definitely the part played in it by Thomas Cromwell. Much has been said about the longstanding ambitions on the part of the crown to eliminate rival authorities in the realm: some scholars would judge the break with Rome to be no more than a predictable climax to earlier disputes. Yet while such disputes between monarchy and papacy did now and again occur, and while the 1394 act of praemunire may deserve some claim to have been an early indicator of the policy finally consummated in 1534, it should not be overlooked that at no time did any king of England declare that he wished to rule 'his' Church separated from the papacy at Rome; and those who like to think that Henry VIII was always ready in return for this or that advantage to rescind the break ought to pay better heed to the determination with which the name and place of the pope was eradicated from the consciousness of the people in the first decade of the new dispensation. Before this, lawsuits travelled all the time to and from the Curia, and the law of the English Church was the canon law of the universal Church. Thereafter, the Roman court might not have existed so far as Englishmen were concerned, and doctors of law laboured to rescue a system for use in Church courts which could not be accused of being papal. Against the idea that the break with Rome initiated England's move towards the ultimately Protestant Reformation two kinds of objection have been raised. Some note that the late-medieval heresy of Lollardy, reviving from about 1490 onwards, really anticipated the Reformation proper which therefore cannot be regarded as a major change in England's religion.[19] Others, on the contrary, point out that the move away from the Catholic consensus of the middle ages took very much longer to become effective in the nation than the concept of a religious revolution starting in the 1530s could suppose.[20] It therefore needs stressing that the Protestant Reformation of the sixteenth century represented a very different change in religion from what Lollardy either proclaimed or achieved, and that the prolonged struggle to turn the country predominantly Protestant (a stage probably not attained until the 1580s) in no way detracts from the manifest first efforts of the 1530s to move in that direction.[21] This is not to stress the fact that one of the really attractive things about England and its people is their normal refusal to fall victim to religious fanaticism.

However, did the secular changes of that decade amount to a major reconstruction? Here the problem is complicated by the fact that these changes quite consciously rested upon, and exploited, positions well established in earlier times: they affected the institutions of monarchy,

---

19 J. A. F. Thompson, *The Later Lollards, 1414-1520* (Oxford, 1965); J. F. Davies, *Heresy and Reform in South East England, 1520-1559* (London, 1983); Margaret Aston, *Lollards and Reformers: Images and Literacy in Late Medieval Religion* (London, 1984).

20 Christopher Haigh, ed., *The English Reformation Revised* (Cambridge, 1987); J. J. Scarisbrick, *The Reformation and the English People* (Oxford, 1984).

21 A. G. Dickens, *The English Reformation* (2nd ed., London, 1989).

Parliament and the law, all of which were ancient. All of them, however, received a new dress in the 1530s. The monarchy acquired direct control over the Church, as an institution and as a system of faith; it was equipped with a better organisation engaged in governing the realm, an organisation which gave reality to claims of governance; and all this was achieved without removing medieval safeguards against personal despotism which in other European monarchies were being dismantled. Indeed, constitutional limitations received more precise definition and thus better effect. The chief of them, of course, lay in the fact the king could not make, unmake or alter the laws of the realm except in his role as king-in-Parliament, that is to say in association with the hereditary peers and the elected Commons. The elaboration of rule which characterised the 1530s operated by means of the mixed sovereign rather than the personal monarch: kings ruled in person through their appointed councillors, but under the ultimate sanction of their law-making Parliaments, and even their special powers - their prerogatives - were regarded as defined in the law. And, as we have seen, this Parliament underwent a transformation of some importance, so much so that as early as the reign of Elizabeth the Reformation Parliament could be recognised as starting things anew.[22] It took on competence as well as supremacy over every aspect of the nation's life; membership in it recognised the incorporation of hitherto separate parts of the king's dominions (it looks as though Cromwell hoped to extend this to Ireland but did not get very far); it became a regular law-making machine used by both the king's government and the members of the commonwealth; and for the first

---

[22] See my 'Arthur Hall, Lord Burghley and the Antiquity of Parliament,' *Studies*, iii, 254 ff., esp. 268-9.

time a reforming administration endeavoured to work through a programme of parliamentary legislation requiring extensive preparation and intensive management. In other words, the features that marked the English parliament down to the further era of reform after 1784 then grew out of its medieval prehistory in the course of a very busy decade.

These issues are here important because they must be fundamental to any assessment of Thomas Cromwell's role and achievement. He exercised at least a great measure of authority for not more than eight years; if ever he was influential it was between 1532 and 1540. Now it is plain that that period coincided with the main unfolding of dramatic change, even if much of that change signalled its coming before 1532 and continued to work itself out after 1540. On these grounds I long ago concluded that the peculiar character of the years in question must be ascribed to the particular work of the man who operated in high office at that time and no other, while the reign of Henry VIII before Cromwell's arrival and after his departure bore noticeably different features. I tried to answer the question 'King or Minister?' in favour of the minister,[23] and even though we have since been told that the debate is dead because a good many other people's influence played a crucial role,[24] I do not think that the issue can be so readily dismissed. There has been, I agree, a remarkable revival in the reputation of Henry VIII, rising in some

---

23 'King or Minister? The Man behind the Henrician Reformation,' *Studies*, i, 173-88.

24 J. A. Guy in *Reassessing the Henrician Age*, ed. A. Fox and J. A. Guy (Oxford, 1986), 178.

quarters almost to the level of king-worship, and some
people would, it seems, incline towards crediting him with
the original ideas and particular plans that were so largely
worked out in the 1530s.[25] I must therefore emphasize
again that the problems faced and solved in that decade,
and more particularly the manner in which they were
tackled, do set it clearly apart from the rest of the reign.
I cannot see that it makes sense to see Henry as a
successful statesman in middle life when at other times he
clearly lacked the vision and application required.
Cromwell may not have been the sole agent responsible for
what happened, but he alone was there at the time and
absent before and after. The 1530s were his decade.

Not that this necessarily justifies the extreme respect that at
one time I bestowed on him as the creative statesman
single-handedly responsible for the transformation which
England then underwent. We have learned much in the
forty years since I first formulated my ideas on Cromwell
and his work, and it is certainly necessary to review and
revise assessments made before that additional knowledge
came forth. There is only one new view which seems to
be totally misguided - that which can see only continuity
throughout the sixteenth century, with no major break or
new start in the middle of Henry's reign.[26] The creation
of a national Church under a layman as supreme head, the

---

25 Especially J. J. Scarisbrick in his splendid biography of *Henry VIII*
(London, 1968).

26 See David Starkey's concluding chapter in C. Coleman and D.
Starkey, ed., *Revolution Reassessed* (Oxford, 1986), for this complete
rejection of any sort of 'revolution'. It is not quite clear whether Dr
Starkey meant to extend his interpretation beyond the details of the
administrative system, but he seems to say that he would.

insertion into the system of a sovereign law-making Parliament, the consolidation of diverse members of the commonwealth into a unitary state, and indeed the recasting of the central administration which replaced government by the king by government under the king[27] - all these, with their tenuous prehistory and their shaky aftermaths characterise the age of Thomas Cromwell and make it an age of change sufficient to permit thoughts of revolution.

It therefore becomes very important to understand the man at the centre of affairs. Did Cromwell possess the qualities of mind and will which the role ascribed to him would seem to demand? We have already seen that he arrived at the helm after a very unusual personal history which acquainted him with places, people and affairs not commonly familiar to monarchs and their councillors, and which in particular freed him from the preconceived ideas that usually dominated the minds of such men. But that, of course, is not enough; we need to sort out his positive qualities. Was he the kind of man who would think in terms of fundamental reforms based on fundamental analysis? The Thomas Cromwell that used to be presented by historians certainly was not. They regarded him as Henry VIII's hatchet man, willing to do the dirty work that his master needed but would not dream of undertaking himself, the destroyer of much better men (for instance Thomas More) and great institutions (the monasteries), pragmatic and without wider vision, personally ambitious and greedy for wealth. The most that could be said for

---

27 I was inclined to accept much criticism on this last point until I heard the 'Tudor Revolution in Government' passionately defended by two American colleagues. This made me re-read my first book and I discovered that I had indeed been ready to surrender too soon!

him was that he did his work with great diligence and efficiency; the one thing certain about him was a total absence of religious faith and sincerity. This was how his first modern biographer saw him, applying American highmindedness and social snobbery to this interesting but deplorable upstart.[28] The picture had the advantage that it justified Cromwell's fall and death: whether the actual charges levelled against him were true did not matter so much as seeing the butcher get his comeuppance.

This reading differed widely from some sixteenth-century opinion, especially from the verdict of John Foxe who saw Cromwell as a Protestant hero. Naturally, this could be written off as mere fantasy, especially since the heroic mantle had already been draped, by J. A. Froude and A. F. Pollard, over the shoulders of the king as the author of his own policy. Nowadays, even those who admire or respect King Henry nevertheless recognise that Cromwell, whether originator or tool of policy, possessed a notable intellect and great interest in thinking problems through from first principles.[29] He testified to these characteristics in the preambles he drew for bills in Parliament: it was in effect Cromwell who introduced the long preamble with expositions of policies and principles which characterised government and later also other people's bills down to the great rebellion. His private archive contained stacks of policy papers on the issues of the day - political, ecclesiastical, social - but also a quantity of *belles lettres*, historical essays, discourses of political philosophy,

---

28 Roger Bigelow Merriman, of Harvard University, was all that name and university imply.

29 Details in *Reform and Renewal*.

descriptions of foreign parts, and so forth.[30] His friends
and acquaintances included some of the leading intellectuals
of the day (Sir Thomas Elyot, Sir Thomas Wyatt, Edward
Hall the lawyer and historian, and in earlier days also
Thomas More), and he admired Erasmus sufficiently to
bestow a sizeable gift of money on him, out of the blue.
Around him there gathered a band of younger intellectuals,
anxious to make careers and encouraged to show their
quality in the production of political tracts, and it was
Cromwell who financed William Marshall's important
translation of the fourteenth-century treatise on politics,
Marsiglio of Padua's *Defender of the Peace*. Marsiglio's
championship of a unified state incorporating its Church
had an obvious appeal to Cromwell who either learned here
to dress his policy in a garment of ideas or found the
treatise pleasing because it reflected his own political
philosophy. He knew and read Machiavelli, though he
should not be called a Machiavellian in the old, pejorative
sense; there is no evidence that he had seen *The Prince*
until well on into the 1530s by which time his mind and
policy were settled. But the thing that matters is that in
many ways he was, surprisingly, himself an intellectual in
politics, though also a statesman able to turn the products
of thought and reflection to practical uses.

However, he was not, of course, the only intellectual in
Henrician politics, and this is where a good deal of the
argument over the 'Tudor Revolution' has arisen. Henry
VIII is himself sometimes credited with the ideas behind
the policy that elevated the holder of the 'imperial crown'
to supremacy in the Church, and it is indeed true that he

---

30 Ibid. 13-14.

talked as early as 1516 about having no superior on earth.[31]   However, while such convictions prepared him for the revolutionary policies pursued after 1532 they did not tell him how to frame them, and in the realm of reformist ideas his participation was at best second-hand - accepting other people's lead.   The only direct contribution he made concerned the pamphleteering in support of the divorce from Catherine: here it was he who from the first took his stand on the points of law and Scripture that supposedly made his first marriage invalid and guaranteed a right to settle the issue in England.[32]   He superintended the efforts to collect 'evidence' in support of this position, but when a more revolutionary collection of texts in support of national independence (the 'empire of England') was undertaken he showed an active interest but no initiative.   This dictionary of useful passages called *Collectanea Satis Copiosa* was put together by Edward Foxe and Thomas Cranmer, with the assistance of John Stokesley - all rewarded with bishoprics though their doctrines differed.[33]   These entrepreneurs contributed very significantly to the political philosophy behind the break with Rome, and it was this body of texts that Cromwell had in mind when he introduced the first parliamentary statute separating England from the papacy with a reference to the testimony of historians.   It was also in this act, which prohibited the appealing of lawsuits outside the realm, that

---

31 G. R. Elton, *Reform and Reformation* (London, 1977), 56.

32 Cf. Virginia Murphy's summary of her findings in *The Divorce Tracts of Henry VIII*, ed. E. Surtz and V. Murphy (Angers, 1988).

33   Graham Nicholson, 'The Act of Appeals and the English Reformation,' *Law and Government under the Tudors*, ed. C. Cross et al., 19-30.

he also spoke of England as an empire, an original development from the conventional concept of a personal imperial authority vested in the king. Cranmer seems to have been responsible for canvassing the universities of Europe for verdicts in favour of the position on consanguinity taken up by Henry and his team; the small harvest was put out in a pre-Cromwellian propaganda book first in Latin and then in English.[34] Foxe used the *Collectanea* in 1534 to define the new position of the crown in another propaganda tract,[35] but by then the whole body of ideas had become common property through having been written into the law. Thus at least some of the positive ideas underlying Cromwell's policy were worked out by others, though sometimes with his assistance, and they remained ideas in books until he showed how they could be turned into reality by means of acts of Parliament.

But Parliament was not Thomas Cromwell's invention: in the realm of ideas, it belonged to the common lawyers of whom Cromwell admittedly was one though a long way from being the most professional or most distinguished. That role belonged to Christopher St German, a thinking lawyer already over seventy years old in 1532 whose contribution has been analysed by Dr John Guy in several places. His conclusions may be summarised as demonstrating that St German gathered together well established common-law claims to supremacy over other laws in the realm (especially the canon law) and pointed to

---

34 *Gravissimae Censurae* and *The Determinations of the ... Universities of Italy and France* (both published 1531: *STC* 14286-7).

35 *De Vera Differentia regiae potestatis et ecclesiasticae* (*STC* 11218).

Parliament as the instrument for making these claims real.[36] This line of thought brought him into conflict with Thomas More who thereby proved that being a common lawyer did not determine all a man's attitudes. Guy has also correctly identified St German as the author of a comprehensive reform paper ranging from the provision of a vernacular Bible to a law on poor relief; some of its details reappear in Cromwell's parliamentary programme. The ideas behind the minister's activities were, not surprisingly, floating about in various places, including the heads of the intellectuals whom he attracted to his own entourage and with some of whom he had become familiar during his service under Wolsey. His contacts with St German are poorly documented but must have existed; after all, the lawyer's draft proposals survive because they finished up in Cromwell's archive. In short, the body of ideas underlying the revolution of the 1530s has a mixed prehistory, some of it long and some more recent, none of it the product of one man's mind. Nevertheless, Cromwell's role remains absolutely crucial. He listened and he contributed, but above all he translated ideas into action. It remains true that he and no one else, certainly not the king, provided the driving force behind events.[37]

A similar relationship between ideas and deeds marks Cromwell's other contributions to this revolutionary era.

---

36 J. A. Guy especially in chs. 5 and 8 of *Reassessing the Henrician Age*, and his edition of *Christopher St German on Chancery and Statute* (Selden Society, 1985).

37 This point is obscured in John Guy's otherwise very important analysis of the ideology in question: 'Thomas Cromwell and the Intellectual Origins of the Henrician Revolution,' *Reassessing the Henrician Age*, 151-78.

Inevitably, he was bound to get involved in the problem facing the Church after its reduction to a department of state, an involvement notably signified by his appointment as Henry's vicar-general and vicegerent in spirituals (1535-6). By stages, he became the supreme head's deputy with powers first to visit and ultimate to execute rule in all respects. This involved the setting up of a court to administer both the provinces of the English Church, and though the actual work of visitation, probate jurisdiction, and so forth was carried out by officers Cromwell exercised the general supervisory function customary to him. In particular he found it necessary to instruct the Church in the way it should go, for which reason he issued two sets of Injunctions, in 1536 and 1538, which defined aspects of doctrine, promoted the 'right' kind of preaching, and tried to remove remaining remnants of papal obedience. He also reformed the universities, abolishing the study of the canon law and supporting the humanist ambitions for a better system of instruction which culminated at both Oxford and Cambridge in 1540 in the establishment of regius chairs in divinity, physic (that is medicine), Greek and Hebrew. None of these things were newly thought up, any more than was the creation of new episcopal dioceses (1540) designed to improve the running of the Church, nor was Cromwell always the man who devised what actually happened. His close associate, Thomas Cranmer, proved a very active archbishop of Canterbury. But once again, it was Cromwell whose presence and restless activity ensured that longstanding notions turned into reality.

This fact most obviously applies to the one bit of policy with which his name remained associated for centuries - the dissolution of the monasteries. The attack on them derived from four sources. For the nascent movement towards

Protestantism the monastic orders represented a perversion of Christianity as well as a remaining tie with Rome. For the ardent reformers of society and especially education they signified a reservoir of misapplied resources. To the land-hungry laity they offered hopes of exploitable wealth. But above all, they exercised that same attraction for a crown markedly underfunded in a world of ever increasing commitments and costs. Add to this the monasteries' at best very moderate hold on opinion in general - the idea that the dissolution offended deeply the instincts of the nation is in the main the invention of later generations - and the victims stood exposed. Here again, the policy ultimately carried out had a long prehistory. Erasmus had led the campaign against monks as obscurantists and obstacles to learning. Small institutions had been dissolved by such sound adherents to the old ways as John Fisher and Thomas Wolsey, seeking funds with which to support new schools and colleges. Laymen had lusted after the monastic endowments for at least 150 years. It took Cromwell to gather together all these elements and within four energetic years close down all religious orders and transfer their assets into the hands of the crown. For their administration a new department was set up - the court of Augmentations - which proved remarkably efficient. This drastic clearing away of very ancient institutions naturally caused much anguish and some hardship, but it was carried out with surprising consideration. A few recalcitrant abbots and priors did suffer death, and their fate certainly stains the achievement indelibly. But pensions were paid to all those ejected, the Augmentations serviced the debts owed by the monasteries, something like a fifth of the yield was redirected into the Church to support educational and diocesan reform. Some of the lands had to be redistributed at once to satisfy the claims of those (including Cromwell himself) on whose services the king depended, but the massive redistribution out of royal hands did not happen until Cromwell was gone and resulted from expensive policies in war and palace-building which he had managed to keep under control. Whatever else may be thought of the dissolution, it was an administrative triumph highly descriptive of Cromwell's manner of government. And, typically too, he had first instituted a census of all ecclesiastical property, the *Valor Ecclesiasticus* which provided detailed knowledge of what the Church owned. Historians have never ceased to be grateful for this undertaking, as they have also been grateful to Cromwell for introducing parish registers of births, marriages and deaths (1538).

Mention of the Augmentations raises the question of Cromwell's administrative reforms. Some forty years ago I argued that he deliberately set out to terminate a system of government which had regularly relied on the royal Household to supply both administrative personnel and organisation to supplement, and commonly to outrank, established agencies that had (as the phrase went) gone out of court. Instead, Cromwell organised the financial administration in institutions removed from the royal financial agency, the king's Chamber; he turned the king's principal secretary from a private household officer into the chief national executive; and especially he reorganised the large and varied king's Council by restricting authority and activity to a group of leading administrators properly to be called the Privy Council.[38] My original version of this story unquestionably ignored circumstances limiting Cromwell's freedom of action: I now think that I overstated

---

38 This, of course, is the subject of my *Tudor Revolution in Government*.

his systematic approach to the problems and represented him as newly creating a structure of government as though he possessed the powers of a god. I would certainly now agree that he worked in a piecemeal fashion, tackling problems as they arose and called for solution, and I entirely agree that in this field as in every other his premature and sudden removal left the work unfinished. But despite doubts cast on this, I still see him working in effect to a master plan: confronted by the needs for administrative efficiency and effectiveness, he promoted measures which incorporated the principle of national against Household government and relied on a bureaucratic organisation relatively independent of personal relationships. Here, too, of course, he employed tried methods; he did not invent the use of established national departments nor has anyone ever suggested that he did. The point is rather that he tried to put an end to the practice of rivalling that sector of government with temporary structures built up within the king's entourage.

This interpretation has been much questioned and in particular has been attacked on two fronts. It is argued that the emergence and development of the king's Privy Chamber in the reigns of Henry VII and Henry VIII perpetuated the dominance of court and Household in the government of the nation,[39] and it has been maintained that the Privy Council emerged in spite of Cromwell rather

---

39 See David Starkey's work, esp. in *Revolution Reassessed*, ch. 2, and his introduction to *The English Court from the Wars of the Roses to the Civil War* (London, 1987).

than through his efforts.[40]   As to the first, it should be
noted that Cromwell's reforming and reorganising activity
extended also to the royal Household and the Privy
Chamber; he turned the latter into a regular spending
department responsible for the monarch's personal needs,
while remitting the covering of the so-to-speak national
expenditure to the Exchequer, the Augmentations, and the
other finance courts; after further reorganisation in 1554,
the reformed Exchequer covered the lot, with the
Household altogether confined to the immediate needs of
king and court.[41]   As for the Council, it is perfectly true
that the Privy Council which organised its business in 1540
looks very like a reform proposed but not carried out by
Wolsey in 1526, but it looks very different from the
variable 'inner ring' that is visible at times in the large old
Council down to the mid-1530s. The crucial points have
been acknowledged by my critics. After 1536, when the
accidental survival of copies of Council letters provides
evidence of a newly restricted membership, we encounter
a clerk newly appointed for the Privy Council and the
mention of councillors expressly not of the Privy Council:
that is, institutional change had taken place. The argument
that it cannot have been guided by Cromwell, even though
we know that he had for some time been contemplating
Council reform, is interesting: it holds that surely he would
not have limited his own freedom of action by giving

---

40   John Guy in *Revolution Reassessed*, ch. 3, and his study of the
Council seen as an instrument for limiting monarchic freedom *Reassessing
the Henrician Age*, ch. 6; the second is interesting and in the main
persuasive but not really relevant to the setting up of a Privy Council
committed to service of the crown.

41   Cf. *Tudor Revolution in Government*, ch. 6, and my review of
Starkey's book in *Hist. Journal* 31 (1988), 425-34.

possible opponents an effective place in government. This quite mistakes the kind of mind he brought to such matters, the kind of mind common among his kind: they reform for the future and the use of their successors, while keeping the better system under effective personal control while they are there.[42] This is what Cromwell did between 1536 and 1540, and this is why his departure necessitated a fresh revision of the Council late in 1540. A by-product of Cromwell's work on the Council was the final settlement of the conciliar courts of Star Chamber and Requests, also foreshadowed by Wolsey but left undone.

So Cromwell was a principled reformer of everything that came within his purview, using existing structures and practices as well as earlier schemes but giving them positive reality derived from consistent principles of efficiency. He did not have time to transform everything in the realm (a fact oddly used on occasion to deny that he transformed anything); considering the time available and the many calls on his labours, he achieved a surprising amount and mapped out lines to be followed by later successors, especially William Cecil under Elizabeth. One thing he could not alter because the task was too enormous and also, as it turned out, not yet necessary: he did not affect the methods by which the centre secured support and action in the provinces. He faced the problem when he began to enforce obedience to the new order in state and Church, and he used the established method of working through the men governing shires and boroughs throughout

---

42 Here I speak from personal experience in administration.

the realm.[43] Even here he did some things to improve the machinery. He gave better shape to the local councils charged with superintending the northern counties and those over against Wales, and he set up a similar though short-lived body to attend to the south-west. He also intensified the normal contacts between centre and extremities by his tireless supervision of what was going on, backed by a stream of informative and exhortatory circulars as well as careful propaganda. But the reform of the system of local government from what the middle ages had handed on waited for the nineteenth century, mainly because the English royal administration already held the realm together more efficiently than was managed by any other West-European monarchy.

V

Behind all these positive attentions to the problems of society there lurks the question of Cromwell's religious faith. In the age of the early Reformation, the one position no one could adopt was genuine indifference to the Christian faith: a man's belief might vary along a scale of intensity, but in essence he found that he had to choose between standing by tradition and favouring innovation. Cromwell, with his automatic reaction to everything he came across, was bound to favour reform, and it would seem that he moved by stages from conventional traditional beliefs to a degree of Protestantism, though he probably never became quite that champion of the new faith that such admirers as John Foxe saw him as. Apart from

---

43 Cf. my *Policy and Police*, and Mary L. Robertson, 'Thomas Cromwell's Management of West Country Government,' *Hist. Journal* 32 (1989), 793-816.

everything else, he had to watch his step in the service of a monarch who abominated Luther and resisted doctrinal change; as he explained to some German envoys in 1538, he inclined to their faith but 'as the world stood, would believe even as his master the king believed'.[44] In actual fact, he was by this time already somewhat out of step. His close association with Cranmer, some of the details of his Injunctions, and his contributions to the debates that produced the formulary known as *The Bishops' Book* (1537), all witness to an increasing adoption of Lutheran tenets on the doctrine of salvation. Above all, he actively forwarded the fortunes of reforming preachers and secured episcopal appointment for such radicals as Hugh Latimer, Nicholas Shaxton, John Hilsey and George Brown; he favoured advanced preachers especially in London;[45] and his religious attitudes lay at the heart of the unrelenting hostility felt for him by such conservatives as Stephen Gardiner and John Stokesley, bishops of Winchester and London. But the essence of Cromwell's position consisted in moderation: he believed in the middle way between the extremes available and he wished to proclaim it, that *via media* that became a typical slogan of developed Anglicanism.[46]

---

44 Merriman, i, 279. On Henry VIII and the holding off of Luther see my 'England und die oberdeutsche Reform,' *Studies*, iii, 321-31.

45 Susan Brigden, *London and the Reformation* (Oxford, 1989), chs. 4 and 6.

46 My *Reform and Renewal*, 51, and cf. Cromwell's speech in the Lords in 1540 (*Lords Journals*, i, 128-9) which anticipated Henry VIII's better known one of 1545 in its praise of the middle way.

VI

Cromwell carried out his life's work in the face of much hatred and without any sort of power base in the political structure of the day. He had his friends, though not many, and while he held power he naturally commanded a good deal of ready support, but the truth remained that he totally depended on Henry's continued trust in his services and usefulness. He himself tried hard to preserve balance and legality in enforcing the new order; he followed the law, and the old legend of his coldblooded ruthlessness should be buried.[47]   The king, selfrighteous and volatile, was another matter: Henry never hesitated when blood was to be shed, though he made sure that the blame would attach to a ministerial scapegoat. It was Henry, not Cromwell, who determined to destroy Anne Boleyn and her friends in 1536,[48] and who decided to wipe out the Yorkist remnants gathered round the Courtenays and Poles in 1538. But the world at large readily accepted the offer of a faithful minister as the alleged cause of the disasters which he was obliged to manage for his master. Cromwell made enemies because he was an upstart rising into the peerage, and though he does not seem to have been particularly greedy he certainly gathered a considerable amount of landed wealth. By 1538 he knew that his life and fortunes could end at a blow if Henry decided that his own image would be best protected by sacrificing Cromwell, and he took

---

47 See *Policy and Police*.

48 It now looks as though Henry felt convinced that Anne had broken her marriage vows because the still-born child (January 1536) would have been proof of God's displeasure if he had been the father: Retha M. Warnicke, *The Rise and Fall of Anne Boleyn* (Cambridge, 1989), ch. 8.

38

some steps to secure the future of his sole surviving child, the very uninteresting Gregory.[49] And by this time he was far too committed a Protestant to feel sure of the king's support.

The conflagration that destroyed Cromwell began in 1538, as Henry sought for a fourth wife; Jane Seymour, Anne's successor, having died in childbirth the year before. England was facing a genuine crisis at this point because the two European powers - the French and the Habsburg monarchies - had temporarily come to terms, an agreement which threatened schismatic England with vengeful moves in support of the papacy and the memory of the emperor's discarded aunt. It was at this point that Cromwell for the first time initiated a foreign policy of his own: he wished to restore the balance by forming an alliance in northern Europe to end England's isolation. However, the two specific steps taken led to disaster. Henry put the kibosh on Cromwell's attempts to ally with Lutheran princes, and though he accepted his vicegerent's suggestion of Anne, princess of Cleves, for his fourth wife he hated the sight of her as soon as they met.

The story of Cromwell's fall remains full of uncertainties, the more so because it followed upon highly successful moves to restore a much shaken position. In the Parliament of 1539 Cromwell (and Cranmer) had suffered a major defeat signalled by the act of six articles with its return to total conservatism in religion, but they had given in in time, and when the Parliament reconvened in April

---

[49] The important succession went through Cromwell's nephew Richard Williams who adopted his uncle's name and became the ancestor of the Cromwells of Hinchinbrook.

1540 Cromwell appeared to be in command once again. In that month he was created earl of Essex and great chamberlain of England, a final promotion which infuriated the older nobility led by Thomas Howard, duke of Norfolk. Trouble arose over the reckless behaviour of some radical clergy, but again Cromwell appeared to have ridden out that storm and was soon turning upon some of his known enemies. The blow fell, not entirely without warning inasmuch as Henry's dissatisfaction with Anne of Cleves and with the state of his foreign policy was plain to see, but yet with a suddenness manifestly contrived to prevent Cromwell from once again carrying out his Houdini act. On 10 June 1540 he was arrested at the Council Table and vanished into the Tower; condemned to death without trial, by act of attainder, he lingered a while because Henry wanted his fallen minister's testimony in securing his second divorce; on 28 July, after on the scaffold he firmly denied the charges of treason and heresy which had been brought against him, his head fell.

The inwardness of that tragedy has been read differently by various scholars. Many years ago I suggested that the events constituted a victory for a conspiracy hatched by Norfolk and Gardiner who won Henry over in part because the desired change in foreign policy would be best achieved by swapping horses, and in part because he allowed himself to believe, briefly but long enough, that his vicegerent in spirituals had become an extreme sacramentarian heretic.[50] This view was in effect supported by J. J. Scarisbrick, and it received a degree of support also from the analysis of religious and political upheavals at Calais which drove

---

50 'Thomas Cromwell's Decline and Fall,' in *Studies*, i, 189-230.

Cromwell into false moves of despair.[51] Lately, however, Glyn Redworth has argued that Gardiner, never given to conspiracy, played no part in the drama and that the king was the mover from the beginning, once again using others as a screen behind which he carried out his dirty game.[52] As he notes, the quite ridiculous charges of treason, seemingly arranged with obedient and selfseeking informers from inside the administration, sufficed to bring Cromwell to the edge of disaster, the charges of heresy being added a little later, possibly to satisfy such conscience as the king still possessed. None of these reconstructions lacks verisimilitude, and none can be conclusively proven. What in the end, however, remains is Henry VIII's personal responsibility, whether it sprang from his own private decision or from reaction to other people's insinuations. As he knew soon enough, he had allowed - or contrived - the destruction of the most loyal and ablest servant he had ever had. England survived Henry VIII, but she would have been served better if the king had died and the minister had lived to complete his life's work now left to others to manage and mismanage.

---

51   Scarisbrick, *Henry VIII*; Muriel St Clair Byrne, ed. *The Lisle Correspondence* (Chicago, 1981), vol. 6.

52   G. Redworth, *In Defence of the Church Catholic: the Life of Stephen Gardiner* (Oxford, 1990), ch. 5.

Further Reading

A small selection from a great mass. General introductions are found in John Guy, *Tudor England* (Oxford, 1988), G. R. Elton, *Reform and Reformation: England 1509-1558* (London, 1977), and A. G. Dickens, *The English Reformation* (2nd ed., London, 1989). Two short biographies of Cromwell throw some light: A. G. Dickens, *Thomas Cromwell and the English Reformation* (London, 1959) initiated a better understanding of Cromwell's religion; B. W. Beckingsale, *Thomas Cromwell: Tudor Minister* (London, 1978) is a monument to judiciousness untroubled by acquaintance with the record. In R. B. Merriman's *Life and Letters of Thomas Cromwell* (2 vols, Oxford, 1902) the Life is best ignored, but the Letters - a nearly complete collection of what survives from the enormous quantity that Cromwell wrote - tell much about his use of the language. Other biographies of value deal with Cromwell's master (J. J. Scarisbrick, *Henry VIII*, London, 1968), and with two of his opponents (Richard Marius, *Thomas More*, New York, 1984 [the first dispassionate life]; Glyn Redworth, *In Defence of the Church Catholic: the Life of Stephen Gardiner*, Oxford, 1990 [presents an improbably innocent bishop]). Three books by G. R. Elton investigate the various facets of Cromwell's career: *The Tudor Revolution in Government* (Cambridge, 1953); *Policy and Police: the Enforcement of the Reformation in the Age of Thomas Cromwell* (Cambridge, 1972); *Reform and Renewal: Thomas Cromwell and the Common Weal* (Cambridge, 1973). Other points are discussed in several of G. R. Elton's collected papers: *Studies in Tudor and Stuart Politics and Government* (3 vols, Cambridge 1974, 1983). Doubts and revisions are collected in two volumes of essays: *Revolution Reassessed: Revisions in the History of Tudor Government and Administration*, ed. C. Coleman and D. R. Starkey (Oxford, 1986); *Reassessing the Henrician Age:*

Humanism, Politics and Reform 1500-1550, ed. A. G. Fox and J. A. Guy (Oxford, 1986). Also very useful: Stanford E. Lehmberg, *The Reformation Parliament 1529-1536* (Cambridge, 1970) and *The Later Parliaments of Henry VIII 1536-1547* (Cambridge, 1977).

BIBLIOGRAPHY OF THE WRITINGS OF G. R. ELTON, 1946-1990

Abbreviations

ARG   *Archiv für reformationsgeschichte*
BIHR   *Bulletin of the Institute of Historical Research*
CHJ   *Cambridge Historical Journal*
EcHR   *Economic History Review*
EHR   *English Historical Review*
HJ   *Historical Journal*
JEH   *Journal of Ecclesiastical History*
P & P   *Past and Present*
TLS   *Times Literary Supplement*
TRHS   *Transactions of the Royal Historical Society*

BOOKS AND ARTICLES

1946

'The date of Caesar's Gallic proconsulate', *Journal of Roman Studies* 36, 18-42.

1949

'Two unpublished letters of Thomas Cromwell', *BIHR* 22, 35-7.
'The evolution of a Reformation statute', *EHR*, 64, 174-97.

Bibliography of the writings of G. R. Elton

1950

'A note on the First Act of Annates', *BIHR* 23, 203-5.

1951

'Thomas Cromwell's decline and fall', *CHJ* 10,150-85.
'The Commons' Supplication of 1532: parliamentary manoeuvres in the reign of Henry VIII', *EHR* 66, 507-34.

1952

'Parliamentary drafts 1529-40', *BIHR* 25, 117-32.
'The Sixteenth Century' in *Annual Bulletin of Historical Literature* (Historical Association).

1953

The Tudor Revolution in Government: Administrative Changes in the Reign of Henry VIII (Cambridge University Press).
'An early Tudor poor law', *EcHR* 2nd series, 6, 55-67.
'The Sixteenth Century' in *Annual Bulletin of Historical Literature* (Historical Association).

1954

'A further note on parliamentary drafts in the reign of Henry VIII', *BIHR* 27, 198-200.
'Informing for profit: a sidelight on Tudor methods of law-enforcement', *CHJ* 11, 149-67.
'King or minister? The man behind the Henrician Reformation', *History* 39, 216-32.

Bibliography of the writings of G. R. Elton

'The Sixteenth Century' in *Annual Bulletin of Historical Literature* (Historical Association).

1955

England Under the Tudors (London: Methuen).
'The Sixteenth Century' in *Annual Bulletin of Historical Literature* Historical Association).

1956

'Thomas Cromwell', *History Today* (August).
'The quondam of Rievaulx', *JEH* 7, 45-60.
'Fifty years of Tudor history at London', *TLS* (6 Jan.).
'The political creed of Thomas Cromwell', *TRHS* 5th series, 6, 69-92.
'The Sixteenth Century' in *Annual Bulletin of Historical Literature* (Historical Association).

1958

(ed.) *The New Cambridge Modern History*, vol. II: *The Reformation* (Cambridge University Press).
Star Chamber Stories (London: Methuen),
'Henry VII: rapacity and remorse', *HJ* I, 21-39.

1959

'The records of the conciliar courts in the 16th century', *The Amateur Historian* 4, 89-94.

Bibliography of the writings of G. R. Elton

1960

The Tudor Constitution: Documents and Commentary (Cambridge University Press).
'Henry VIII's Act of Proclamations', *EHR* 75, 208-22.

1961

'The Elizabethan Exchequer: war in the Receipt,' in *Elizabethan Government and Society*, ed. S. T. Bindoff, J. Hurstfield, C. H. Williams (London: Athlone Press), pp. 213-48.
'State planning in early Tudor England', *EcHR* 2nd series, 13, 433-9.
'Henry VII: a restatement', *HJ* 4,1-29.
'Stuart Government', *P & P* 20,76-82.

1962

The Reformation (BBC Publications).
Henry VIII: an Essay in Revision (Historical Association, Pamphlet G 51).

1963

Reformation Europe (London: Collins).
(ed.) *Ideas and Institutions in Western Civilization*, vol. III: *Renaissance and Reformation* (New York: Macmillan).
(ed. with G. Kitson Clark) *Guide to the Research Facilities in History in the Universities of Great Britain and Ireland* (Cambridge University Press).
'The teaching of history', *Cambridge Review* 84, 250.

Bibliography of the writings of G. R. Elton

'Anglo-French relations in 1522: a Scottish prisoner of war and his interrogation', *EHR* 78, 310-13.

1964

'The Tudor Revolution: a reply', *P & P* 29, 26-49.

1965

'Why the history of the early Tudor Council remains unwritten', *Annali della Fondazione Italiana per la Storia Amministrativa* I, 268-96.

'A high road to civil war?' *From the Renaissance to the Counter-Reformation: Essays in Honor of Garrett Mattingley*, ed. C. H. Carter (New York: Random House), pp. 325-47.

'The problems and significance of administrative history in the Tudor period', *Journal of British Studies* 4 no. 2, 18-28.

Introduction to J. N. Figgis, *The Divine Right of Kings* (repr. Harper Torchbooks).

Introduction to A. F. Pollard, *Wolsey* (repr. Fontana Library).

'1555: a political retrospect', in *The Reformation Crisis*, ed. J. Hurstfield (London: Arnold).

'Government by edict?', *HJ* 8, 266-71.

'A revolution in Tudor history?' *P & P* 32, 103-9.

1966

Introduction to M. Creighton, *Queen Elizabeth* (repr. Crowell).

Bibliography of the writings of G. R. Elton

1967

The Practice of History (Sydney University Press).
'Thomas More and the opposition to Henry VIII', *Moreana* 15 & 16, 285-303.
(ed.) *Storia del Mondo Moderno*, vol. II.

1968

(ed.) *Ideas and Institutions in Western Civilization: Renaissance and Reformation*, 2nd edn. (New York: Macmillan).
The Future of the Past (Cambridge University Press).
'Thomas More and the opposition to Henry VIII', (repr. from Moreana 15 & 16), *BIHR* 41, 19-34.
'The law of treason in the early Reformation', HJ 11, 211-36.
'Reform by statute: Thomas Starkey's *Dialogue* and Thomas Cromwell's policy', *Proceedings of the British Academy*, 54, 165-88.
Review article on G. E. Aylmer, *The Struggle for the Constitution, Annali della Fondazione Italiana per la Storia Amministrativa* 2, 759-65.
'Interdisciplinary courses', *Cambridge Review* (26 Jan.).
'Graduate studies in the humanities', *Cambridge Review* (18 Oct.).

1969

The Sources of History: England 1200-1640 (London: Sources of History Ltd.).
The Body of the Whole Realm': Parliament and Representation in Medieval and Tudor England (Charlottesville: University Press of Virginia).

Bibliography of the writings of G. R. Elton

'Literaturbericht über die englische Geschichte der Neuzeit', *Historische Zeitschrift*, Sonderheft 3.

'The King of Hearts', *HJ* 12, 158-63.

'The Good Duke', *HJ* 12, 702-6.

'A reply [to a review of *The Practice of History*]', *Journal of Historical Studies*, Winter 1968-9, 49-59.

'Second thoughts on history in the Universities', *History* 54, 60-7.

'Personal view', *The Listener* (27 Mar.).

1970

Political History: Principles and Practice (New York: Basic Books).

Modern Historians on British History 1485-1945: a Critical Bibliography (London: Methuen).

'Reformation in Church and State 1485-1603', *Encyclopaedia Americana* ('England').

'What sort of history should we teach?' *New Movements in the Study and Teaching of History*, ed. M. Ballard (London: Temple Smith), pp. 221-30.

1971

Europa im Zeitalter der Reformation, 2 vols. (Siebenstern).

'Government and society in Renaissance and Reformation Europe', in N. F. Cantor, ed., *Perspectives on the European Past: Conversations with Historians* (New York: Macmillan), pp. 228-51.

'Studying the history of parliament', *British Studies Monitor* 4, 3-12.

'Tudor historians', *The Listener* (30 Sept.).

Bibliography of the writings of G. R. Elton

1972

Policy and Police: the Enforcement of the Reformation in the Age of Thomas Cromwell (Cambridge University Press).
'Thomas More, councillor', *St Thomas More: Action and Contemplation*, ed. R. S. Sylvester (New Haven: Yale University Press), pp. 86-122.
'The rule of law in the sixteenth century', *Tudor Men and Institutions*, ed. A. J. Salvin (Baton Rouge: Louisiana State University Press), pp. 260-84.
'Reply [to J. H. Hexter]', *British Studies Monitor* 3, 16-22.

1973

Reform and Renewal: Thomas Cromwell and the Common Weal (Cambridge University Press).

1974

England under the Tudors, 2nd edn. (London: Methuen).
Studies in Tudor and Stuart Politics and Government, 2 vols. (Cambridge University Press).
La Europa de la Reforma (Siglo Veintuino).
Political History: Japanese translation.
'Consultants' Report on Graduate Programs in History in the Province of Ontario. 'Thomas Cranmer', 'Thomas Cromwell', 'Henry VIII' in *Encyclopaedia Britannica* (15th edn.).
'The early Journals of the House of Lords', *EHR* 89, 481-512.
'Tudor Politics: the points of contact. I. Parliament', *TRHS* 5th series, 24, 183-200.

Bibliography of the writings of G. R. Elton

1975

'Taxation for peace and war in early Tudor England', *War and Economic Development: Essays in Memory of David Joslin*, ed. J. M. Winter (Cambridge University Press), pp. 33-48.

'Thomas Cromwell and reform', *Annual Report of the Friends of Lambeth Library*.

'Tudor Politics: the points of contact. II The Council', *TRHS* 5th series, 25, 195-211.

1976

Ideas and Institutions in Western Civilisation, vol. III: Renaissance and Reformation, 3rd edn. (New York: Macmillan).

'Publishing history', *TLS* (25 June).

'Tudor Politics: the points of contact. III The Court', *TRHS* 5th series, 26, 211-28.

(ed.) *Annual Bibliography of British and Irish History: Publications for 1975* (Brighton: Harvester Press).

1977

Reform and Reformation: England 1509-1558 (London: Arnold).

'Introduction: crime and the historian', in J. S. Cockburn, ed., *Crime in England 1550-1800* (London: Methuen), pp. 1-14.

'Thomas Cromwell *redivivus*', *ARG* 68, 192-208.

'A new venture in history publishing', *British Book News* (December).

'Mid-Tudor finance', *HJ* 20, 737-40.

Bibliography of the writings of G. R. Elton

'The historian's social function', *TRHS* 5th series, 27, 197-211.

(ed.) *Annual Bibliography and Irish History: Publications for 1976* (Brighton: Harvester Press).

1978

'The sessional printing of statutes, 1484-1547', in *Wealth and Power in Tudor England: Essays Presented to S. T. Bindoff*, eds. E. W. Ives, R. J. Knecht and J. J. Scarisbrick (London Athlone Press), pp. 68-86.

'England und die oberdeutsche Reformation,' *Zeitschrift für Kirchengeschichte*, 3-11.

(ed.) *Annual Bibliography of British and Irish History: Publications for 1977* (Brighton: Harvester Press).

1979

English Law in the Sixteenth Century: Reform in an Age of Change (London: Selden Society).

'Reform and the "Commonwealth-Men" of Edward VI's reign', in *The English Commonwealth 1547-1640: Essays in Politics and Society presented to Joel Hurstfield*, eds. P. Clark, A. G. R. Smith and N. Tyacke (Leicester University Press), pp. 23-38.

'The Rolls of Parliament 1449-1547', *HJ* 22, 1-29.

'Parliament in the sixteenth century: function and fortunes', *HJ* 22, 255-78.

'England and the continent in the sixteenth century', *Studies in Church History*, Subsidia 2, ed. D. Baker (Oxford: Blackwell), pp. 1-16.

'Catching up British history: I Tudors and early Stuarts', *TLS* (23 Nov.).

Bibliography of the writings of G. R. Elton

(ed.) *Annual Bibliography of British and Irish history: Publications for 1978* (Brighton: Harvester Press).

1980

'The real Thomas More?' in *Reformation Principle and Practice: Essays in Honour of A. G. Dickens*, ed. P. N. Brooks (London: Scolar Press), pp. 21-31.

'Politics and the Pilgrimage of Grace', in *After the Reformation: Essays in Honor of J. H. Hexter*, ed. B. Malament (Philadelphia: University of Pennsylvania Press), pp. 25-56.

'Enacting clauses and legislative initiative 1559-1581', *BIHR* 53, 183-91.

(ed.) *Annual Bibliography of British and Irish History: Publications for 1979* (Brighton: Harvester Press).

1981

'Cranmer, Thomas', *Theologische Realenzykopädie*, vol. VIII.

'Arthur Hall, Lord Burghley and the antiquity of parliament', in *History and Imagination: Essays in Honour of H. R. Trevor-Roper*, eds. H. Lloyd-Jones, V. Pearl and B. Worden (London: Duckworth), pp. 83-103.

'Thomas More', in *Gestalten der Kirchengeschichte, Reformationzeit* I, ed. M. Greschat (Stuttgart: Kohlhammer), pp. 89-103.

(ed.) *Annual Bibliography of British and Irish History: publications for 1980* (Brighton: Harvester Press).

Bibliography of the writings of G. R. Elton

1982

The Tudor Constitution, 2nd edn. (Cambridge University Press).
Europa im Zeitalter der Reformation 1517-1559, 2nd edn. (Munich: C. H. Beck).
'Contentment and discontent on the eve of colonization', in *Early Maryland in a Wider World*, ed. D. B. Quinn (Detroit: Wayne State University Press), 105-18.
(ed.) *Annual Bibliography of British and Irish History: Publications for 1981* (Brighton: Harvester Press).
A Europa durante a Reforma 1517-1559 (Lisbon: Editorial Presença).
'Elisabeth I', *Theologische Realenzykopädie*, vol. IX.

1983

Studies in Tudor and Stuart Politics, vol. III (Cambridge University Press).
England unter den Tudors (München: Callwey).
'Kann man sich auf Shakespeare verlassen? Das 15. Jahrhundert bei Shakespeare und in der Wirklichkeit', *Deutsche Shakespeare-Gesellschaft West: Jahrbuch 1983*, 27-39.
'The English parliament in the sixteenth century: estates and statutes ', A. Cosgrove, J. I. McGuire, eds., *Parliament and Community*, Historical Studies, 16 (Dublin: Appletree Press), pp. 69-95.
'Historians against History', *Cambridge Review* 104, 203-5.
With R. W. Fogel, *Which Way to the Past? Two Views of History* (New Haven and London: Yale University Press).
(ed.) *Annual Bibliography of British and Irish History: Publications for 1982* (Brighton: Harvester Press).

Bibliography of the writings of G. R. Elton

1984

The History of England (Cambridge University Press).
'Herbert Butterfield and the study of history', *HJ* 27, 729-43.
'Commemorating Luther', *JEH* 35, 614-19.
'Wales in parliament, 1542-1581', in *Welsh Society and Nationhood: Historical Essays presented to Glanmor Williams*, eds. R. R. Davies, R. A. Griffiths, I. G. Jones, K. O. Morgan (Cardiff: University of Wales Press), pp. 108-21.
'Lex terrae victrix: Der Rechtstreit in der englischen Frühreformation', *Zeitschrift der Savigny-Stiftung* 100, 217-36.
'Parliament', in C. A. Haigh, ed., *The Reign of Elizabeth I* (London: Macmillan), pp. 79-100.
'Persecution and toleration in the English Reformation', *Studies in Church History*, 21, ed. W. J. Sheils (Oxford: Blackwell), pp. 163-87.
'Auseinandersetzung und Zusammenarbeit zwischen Renaissance und Reformation in England', *Renaissance-Reformation: Gegensätze und Gemeinsamkeiten*, ed. A. Buck (Wolfenbüttler Abhandlungen 5: Wiesbaden: Harrassowitz), pp. 217-25.
(ed.) *Annual Bibliography of British and Irish History: Publications for 1983* (Brighton: Harvester press).

1985

F. W. Maitland (London: Weidenfeld).
'The State: government and politics under Elizabeth and James', in J. W. Andrews, ed., *William Shakespeare: his World, his Work, his Influence*, 3 vols. (New York: Scribner's), pp. 1-19.

Bibliography of the writings of G. R. Elton

'Once more, the History Faculty Building', *Cambridge Review* 106, 89-90.
(ed.) *Annual Bibliography of British and Irish History: Publications for 1984* (Brighton: Harvester press).
'Political History', *History Today* (Jan.), 11-12.
'Europe and the Reformation, 'in *History, Society and the Churches: Essays in Honour of Owen Chadwick*, eds. D. Beales and G. Best (Cambridge University Press), pp. 89-104.
'History according to St Joan', *The American Scholar* (autumn number).
'Luther and society', *Lutherjahrbuch* 52, 213-19.
'King Henry VII', *Transactions of the Hon. Society of Cymmrodorion*, 131-45.

1986

The Parliament of England 1559-1581 (Cambridge University Press).
'Revisionism Reassessed: the Tudor Revolution a Generation later', *Encounter* (July/Aug.), 37-42.
'English national selfconsciousness and the parliament in the 16th century', in *Nationalismus in vorindustrieller Zeit*, ed. O. Dann (Munich: Oldenbourg), pp. 73-82.
'Piscatorial politics in the early parliament of Elizabeth I', in *Business Life and Public Policy: Essays in Honour of D. C. Coleman*, eds. N. McKendrick and R. B. Outhwaite (Cambridge University Press), pp. 1-20.
'Die europäische Reformation: mit oder ohne Luther?', in *Martin Luther: Probleme seiner Zeit*, eds. V. Press and D. Stievermann (Stuttgart: Klett-Cotta), pp. 43-57.
'Neale, Sir John Ernest', *Dictionary of National Biography 1971-80*, pp. 623-4.

Bibliography of the writings of G. R. Elton

1987

'A new age of reform', *Hist. Journal* 30, 709-16.

1988

'Tudor Government', *Hist. Journal* 31, 425-34.
'Legal History', in *Blackwell's Dictionary of Historians*.

1989

'The Policy of Princes', *History Sixth*, vol. 4.
'Centenary Celebrations', *Cambridge Review*.

1990

'Humanism in England', *The Impact of Humanism on Western Europe* (ed. A. Goodman and A. MacKay), 259-78.
'Lex terrae victrix: the triumph of parliamentary law in the sixteenth century', *The Parliaments of Elizabethan England* (ed. D. M. Dean and N. Jones), 15-36.
'Thomas More and Thomas Cromwell', *Reformation, Humanism, and "Revolution"* (ed. G. J. Schochet), 95-110.
'Lancelot Andrews', *Pembroke College Cambridge Annual Gazette*.
(ed.) *New Cambridge Modern History* vol. 2, 2nd ed.

ACKNOWLEDGEMENTS

To the Frick Collection, New York
    for kind permission to reproduce the portrait of
    Thomas Cromwell.

To Carolyn Shepherd of The Wordsmith Group, Chester
    for setting and design.

To Roderick Boyd of The Ipswich Book Company
    for printing, production and cover design.